IRish TOASTS

Designed by Tony and Penny Mills

irish TOASTS

Tara

This edition published and distributed by Tara, 1999

Tara is an imprint of Parragon

Parragon
Queen Street House
4 Queen Street
Bath BA1 1HE

Produced by Magpie Books, an imprint of
Robinson Publishing Ltd, London

ISBN 1 90287 905 8

A copy of the British Library Cataloguing-in-Publication Data is available
from the British Library

Printed in China

ACKNOWLEDGEMENTS

Pictures on pp 2, 23, 25, 27, 47, 49 have been very kindly supplied by
Celia Haddon. The picture on p 41 is a detail from *Snapp Apple Night* by
Daniel Maclise (1806–70), by courtesy of Phillips, Bridgeman Art
Library; that on p 45 is *The Linley Sisters* (Mrs Sheridan and MrsTickell) by
Thomas Gainsborough (1727–88), by courtesy of the Dulwich Picture
Gallery, Bridgeman Art Library.
We have been unable to trace the owners of certain copyrights and beg
forgiveness of anyone whose rights have been overlooked.

CONTENTS

INTRODUCTION

Guinness, and Irish stout generally, are famous the whole world over, and no mental picture of Ireland is complete without the vision of the pubs of Dublin: outside, warm lights shining on the damp evening streets, and within, every subject under the sun being discussed with much wit and some wisdom.

Whiskey is thought to have been first distilled in the Middle Ages – it was known as *usqebagh*, the water of life, as it was credited with health-giving properties. It has been said that whiskey is not merely 'food and drink' but 'food and clothes' to an Irishman.

There are toasts in this book for all occasions on which these sovereign delights may be consumed.

TO POSTERITY

May your children's children be
As multitudinous as the sands of the sea.

May there be a generation of children
On the children of your children.

Here's to health and prosperity,
To you and all your posterity.
And them that doesn't drink with sincerity,
That they may be damned for all eternity.

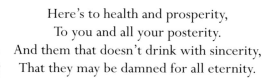

TO LONGEVITY . . .

May you live to be a hundred years,
With one extra year to repent!

May you live on to a hundred and five,
And, if not your business, your pleasure
thrive!

. . . AND HOW TO COPE WITH IT

You're not as young as you used to be.
But . . .
You're not as old as you're going to be.
So drink up!

What is age but something to count?
Some people fight it as if climbing
the mount.
I choose to live with dignity and grace,
And offer a drink to all in this place!

To Age! To Age! Why does one care?
As the wrinkles grow longer grey
graces your hair.
Life should be simple because when
push comes to shove,
The only one counting is the
Good Lord above!

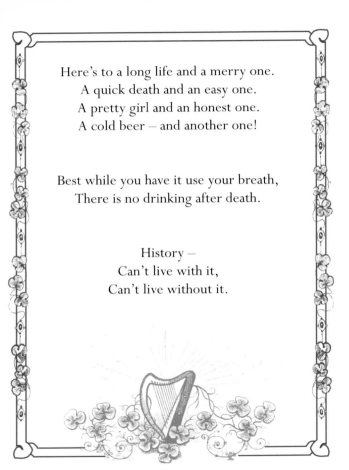

Here's to a long life and a merry one.
A quick death and an easy one.
A pretty girl and an honest one.
A cold beer – and another one!

Best while you have it use your breath,
There is no drinking after death.

History –
Can't live with it,
Can't live without it.

Lifestyle Toasts

May you live all the days of your life.

JONATHAN SWIFT

Here's that we may always have
A clean shirt,
A clean conscience,
And a pound in your pocket.

"St. Patrick's Day   in the Morning"

May you . . .
Work like you don't need the money,
Make friends like you've never been hurt,
Dance like no one is watching,
Make love like it's being filmed,
And drink like a true Irishman.

Here's to a fellow who smiles
When life runs along like a song.
And here's to the lad who can smile
When everything goes dead wrong.

May the Lord keep you in His hand,
And never close His fist too tight.

May you be poor in misfortune,
Rich in blessings,
Slow to make enemies,
And quick to make friends.

May the Good Lord take a liking to you,
But not too soon!

May the grass grow long on the road to
Hell for want of use.

TO EXCESS

When we drink, we get drunk.
When we get drunk, we fall asleep.
When we fall asleep, we commit no sin.
When we commit no sin, we go to Heaven.
So, let's all get drunk and go to Heaven!

An Irishman is never drunk as long as
He can hold onto one blade of grass and not
Fall off the face of the earth!

14

Be one who drinks the finest of ales,
Every day without fail.
Even when you have drank enough,
Remember that ale is wonderful stuff.

No creature ever invented anything
as bad as drunkenness,
Or as good as drink.

Here's to a temperance supper,
With water in glasses tall,
And coffee and tea to end with –
And me not there at all!

'Twas an evening in November,
As I very well remember,
I was strolling down the street in drunken
pride.
But my knees were all aflutter,
So I landed in the gutter,
And a pig came up and lay down by my side.
Yes, I lay there in the gutter,
Thinking thoughts I could not utter,
When a colleen passing by did softly say,
"You can tell a man that boozes
By the company he chooses."
At that the pig got up and walked away!

TO BEER

Madiera costs too much,
Whiskey's too rough,
Brandy puts big mouths in gear.
This little refrain,
Should help to explain,
Why it's better to order a beer!

When money's tight and hard to get,
and your horse is also ran,
When all you have is a heap of debt,
a pint of plain
is your only man.

For every wound, a balm.
For every sorrow, cheer.
For every storm, a calm.
For every thirst, a beer.

"For we could not now take time for further
search (to land our ship) our victuals being
much spent, especially our Beere."

SHIP'S LOG OF
THE MAYFLOWER

WINE & SPIRITS

Here's champagne to your real friends,
And real pain to your sham friends!

I love everything that is old;
old friends, old times, old manners,
old books, old wines.

OLIVER GOLDSMITH

Blessings on the man
who brought the still to Ireland.

May whiskey, by sea or by land, in all
weather,
Be never denied to the children of care.

Love and whiskey both,
Rejoice an honest fellow.

Mother's in the kitchen washing out the jugs,
Sister's in the pantry bottling the suds,
Father's in the cellar mixin' up the hops,
Johnny's on the front porch watchin' for the cops.

PROHIBITION SONG

SPORTING TOASTS

The health of the salmon
and of the trout.

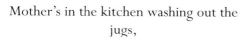

May there be a fox on your fishing hook,
And a hare on your bait.
And may you kill no fish,
Until St Brigid's Day.

well wishes

May the most you wish for
Be the least you get.

For each petal on the shamrock,
This brings a wish your way –
Good health, good luck, and happiness,
For today and every day.

May you get all your wishes but one,
So you will always have something
to strive for!

HOSPITABLE & FRIENDLY TOASTS

Here's a health to all those that we love,
Here's a health to all those that love us,
Here's a health to all those that love them . . .
        that love those,
        that love them,
        that love those,
        that love us.

Here's a toast to the roast that good
fellowship lends,
With the sparkle of beer and wine.
May its sentiment always be deep,
my friends,
And its taste be equally fine.

May your glass be ever full.
May the roof over your head be always
strong.
And may you be in Heaven half an hour
before
the devil knows you're dead.

31

Forsake not an old friend,
For the new is not comparable to him.
A new friend is as new wine:
When it is old,
Thou shalt drink it with pleasure.

Here's a toast to your enemies'
enemies!

Who is a friend but someone to toast,
Someone to gibe, someone to roast.
My friends are the best friends,
Loyal, willing and able.

Here's to you and yours,
And to mine and ours.
And if mine and ours
Ever come across to you and yours,
I hope you and yours will do
As much for mine and ours,
As mine and ours have done
For you and yours!

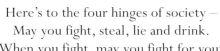

Here's to the four hinges of society –
May you fight, steal, lie and drink.
When you fight, may you fight for your
country.
When you steal, may you steal away from
bad company.
When you lie, may you lie at the side of
your sweetheart.
And when you drink, may you drink
with me.

IN THE PUB

When the hour is nigh me,
Let me in a tavern die
With a tankard by me.

TWELFTH CENTURY

I'll have what the man on
the floor's having!

Now let's get to drinking.
Glasses off the table!

Here's to bein' single . . .
Drinkin' doubles . . .
And seein' triple!

the LaDies

Here's to Eileen O'Hara,
For her life it held no terror.
Born a virgin,
Died a virgin.
No runs, no hits, no errors.

Here's to the women in the
high-heeled shoes,
Who smoke men's fags and drink
men's booze.

Here's to women's kisses,
and to whiskey, amber clear;
Not as sweet as a woman's kiss,
but a damn sight more sincere!

Here's to beefsteak when you're hungry,
Whiskey when you're dry,
All the women you'll ever want,
And Heaven when you die.

"LET THE TOAST PASS"

Here's to the maiden of bashful fifteen,
   Here's to the widow of fifty.
Here's to the flaunting, extravagant queen,
   And here's to the housewife that's
      thrifty.

CHORUS
Let the toast pass,
Drink to the lass,
I'll warrant she'll prove an excuse
for the glass.

Here's to the charmer whose dimples
  we prize,
    Now to the maid who has none, sir.
Here's to the girl with a pair of blue eyes,
    And here's to the nymph with but one,
      sir!

Let the toast pass, &C

Here's to the maid with a bosom of snow,
    And to her that's as brown as a berry.
Here's to the wife with a face full of woe,
    And now to the damsel that's merry.

Let the toast pass, &C

For let 'em be clumsy, or let 'em be slim,
  Young or ancient, I care not a feather.
So fill the pint bumper quite up to the
  brim,
  And let us e'en toast them together.

CHORUS
Let the toast pass,
Drink to the lass,
I'll warrant she'll prove an excuse
  for the glass.

RICHARD BRINSLEY SHERIDAN

44

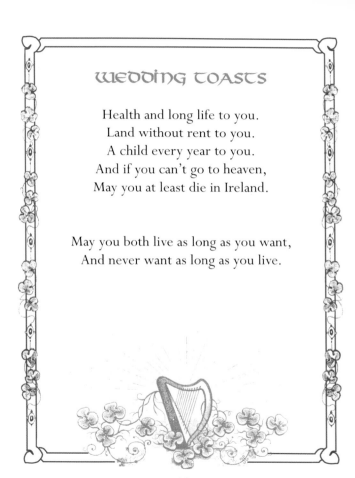

WEDDING TOASTS

Health and long life to you.
Land without rent to you.
A child every year to you.
And if you can't go to heaven,
May you at least die in Ireland.

May you both live as long as you want,
And never want as long as you live.

May you have warm words
on a cold evening,
A full moon on a dark night,
And the road downhill
all the way to your door.

May all your ups and downs
come only in the bedroom!

May you have:
No frost on your spuds,
No worms on your cabbage,
May your goat give plenty of milk.
And if you inherit a donkey,
May she be in foal.

May the joys of today
Be those of tomorrow.
The goblets of life
Hold no dregs of sorrow.

May you be as happy in life as me and eh . . .
what's her name?

As you slide down the bannister of life,
May the splinters never point the
wrong way.

May the roof above us never fall in,
And may the friends gathered below it
never fall out.

May your troubles be less
And your blessings be more.
And nothing but happiness
Come through your door.

CHRISTMAS

A Merry Christmas this December
To a lot of folks I don't remember.

Now, thrice welcome, Christmas!
Which brings us good cheer,
Mince pies and plum pudding –
Strong ale and strong beer!

Here's to holly and ivy hanging up,
And to something wet in
every cup.

IRELAND – NO PLACE LIKE IT

For Dublin hath no sober man,
Or none of milksop thinkers,
And no philosophical fools,
But great and glorious drinkers!

May the enemies of Ireland never
meet a friend.

Here's to the
Shamrock green,
Here's to my
sweet Colleen,
Here's to auld
Ireland so fair,
Loved by her dear
sons everywhere.

To
Greet you
on
St. Patrick's
Day

St Patrick was a gentleman
Who through strategy and stealth
Drove all the snakes from Ireland,
Here's toasting to his health.
But not too many toastings
Lest you lose yourself and then,
Forget the good St Patrick
And see all those snakes again!

May the luck of the Irish
Lead to happiest heights.
And the highway you travel
Be lined with green lights.